C000302565

The Halogen Oven Cookbook

The Halogen Oven Cookbook
Compiled by Paul Jones and Leah Meads
ISBN: 978-0-9551674-4-7

Bookworm of Retford 2009

www.thehalogenovencookbook.co.uk
info@thehalogenovencookbook.co.uk

Cover, logo and photo design: Leah Georgette Photography
Bookworm of Retford
1 Spa Lane
Retford
Nottinghamshire
DN22 6EA

Printed and bound by Burgess Design and Print, Retford

Bookworm of Retford

Contents

Hints and Tips

Whilst we have thoroughly checked our cooking times for our recipes, always ensure food is piping hot before serving. You should also refer to your manufacturer's instructions for operational and maintenance instructions. However, we have a few hints and tips to help you make the most of your Halogen Oven.

★ Time Saving

The main feature of the Halogen Oven is that it reduces cooking times. Most of this time is saved in the preheating stage, as it takes next to no time for the heating element and the rest of the oven to reach the desired temperature. Most of the recipes here are easy to follow and involve mainly one-pot cooking. By the time you have prepared all your ingredients, your oven will be at the required temperature.

★ Using the Cooking Racks

As the heating element is at the top of the oven, the food on the higher cooking rack will cook more quickly than on the bottom cooking rack. The higher rack will cook food in a similar way to a grill; food placed on the lower rack will bake and roast. Vegetables that are to be roasted do not need a cooking rack and can be placed straight onto the base of your Halogen Oven.

★ Finishing Touches

There are many other benefits to using a Halogen Oven aside from the economical and time-saving factors. As the heat comes from above the food, it is great at adding nice crispy, golden finishes to things like pies with mashed potato or pastry toppings. Also, most of the recipes in this book are cooked in just one pot and involve baking, roasting or braising; this often eliminates the need for large amounts of fats like oils and butter, although small amounts of olive oil are used frequently to help prevent food from drying out.

★ Additional Cooking Space

Your Halogen Oven can also be used as an additional cooking space when your normal oven is already full. Why not use it to do the roast potatoes for a Sunday lunch, or broccoli and cauliflower gratin to accompany a casserole?

★ Care of the Heating Element

The heating element is delicate so requires special care. The lid should always be left to cool before cleaning. It shouldn't get too dirty during cooking, so a quick wipe will suffice, but don't rinse it, simply dry with a cloth. Also, when taking the top off the Halogen Oven in order to test the food, simply place it on a suitably sized heat-proof mat. Covering the mat in tinfoil gives added protection.

★ Experiment

The Halogen Oven works in much the same way as a conventional oven: anything that can be baked, roasted, grilled or braised in a conventional oven can be done in the Halogen Oven! Have the confidence to experiment with your cooking as the Halogen Oven is amazingly gentle and does not burn food easily. You can always see what is happening through the glass bowl; just keep testing the food until it is cooked.

★ Useful Accessories

To make using your Halogen Oven even easier, here are some common kitchen accessories that will be very useful:

- Tinfoil (to wrap and steam small portions of vegetables and to protect the top of meat from overcooking)
- Small roasting tin approx 26cm (10 –11 inches)
- Oven-proof casserole dish approx 26cm (10-11 inches)
- A round pizza tray, great for chips and potato wedges and pizzas!, approx 28cm (11 inches)
- Heat-proof mat, on which to stand the lid when it's hot
- Oven gloves: your Halogen Oven will get very hot!
- Tongs for turning food

★ Defrosting

Turn the dial to the 'defrost' or 'thaw' setting. For small items such as bread rolls and sliced bread, set the timer to 5 minutes but keep checking your food regularly. For meat portions and frozen meals set the timer to 10 minutes, adding further minutes as required. Food defrosted in a Halogen Oven may start to get warm and should therefore be cooked immediately after defrosting.

★ Timing guide

Each recipe shows a number of clocks indicating how long it will take to prepare and cook the dish.

30 minutes or less	🕐
1 hour or less	🕐 🕐
Over 1 hour	🕐 🕐 🕐

These recipes have been tested in a 12 litre Halogen Oven. Please ensure you check your manufacturer's guide for preheating times for smaller ovens.

Use these hints and tips as a guide, but always refer to your manufacturer's instructions and ensure food is thoroughly heated before serving.

Don't forget that cooking times will depend on the size and cut of the pieces of meat, poultry, and fish and also by how fresh your ingredients are. You should cook to suit your personal tastes.

Cooking Vegetables

Vegetables are not often the main star of a dish, but if they are not cooked well can ruin an otherwise great meal. By giving yourself plenty of time to prepare them, you can ensure they always cook well and become a regular addition to your Halogen Oven.

Cook vegetables at 200°C on the low rack or on the base of the glass bowl.

★ Small Portions of Vegetables

Small portions of green vegetables can be cooked along with any meat in your cooker. Green vegetables such as peas, green beans or broccoli are best cooked wrapped in tin foil with a tbsp or two of water. This way, they will retain their moisture, colour and nutrients:

The following vegetables are ideally cooked wrapped in tinfoil:

peas	10-15	minutes
broccoli	20	minutes
cauliflower	20	minutes

★ Root Vegetables

Root vegetables such as carrots, swede, parsnips, leeks and celeriac, etc. can be roasted in the bottom of the glass bowl. Simply cut or slice them into bite-sized chunks; the smaller you cut them, the quicker they will cook. However, be careful not to cut them too small or they will lose their texture and shape. Roasting root vegetables like this will take up to an hour; parboiling for 8-10 minutes will reduce the roasting times by approximately 25-30 minutes.

★ Using Olive Oil on your Vegetables

Vegetables such as tomatoes, peppers, red onions and even garlic are at their best when roasted in a little olive oil. Cut them into similar sizes so they cook evenly; toss in a few whole garlic cloves. Leave the skins on the cloves and roast for 20 minutes. When ready, squeeze the garlic out of their skins and serve with meat or fish.

★ Broccoli and Cauliflower Gratin

Cook at 200°C.

Broccoli and cauliflower gratin is really simple. Cut the vegetables into florets and boil for 3 minutes in boiling, salted water. While they are boiling mix 6 tbsp of double cream with 2 egg yolks and set aside. Drain the vegetables and place in a suitably sized heatproof dish; then pour over the cream and egg mixture, season with salt, pepper and Parmesan cheese and bake for 15 minutes or until golden brown and the cheese is bubbling nicely.

★ Jacket Potatoes

Wash and then pierce the potatoes several times with a fork. Cook for 60 minutes at 200°C. After 45 minutes start checking the potatoes to see if they are cooked.

★ Experiment

Use the times given in this book to create your own meal ideas. Prepare all your ingredients, roast your chosen vegetables and then grill your meat on top. The juice from the meat will add a great flavour to the vegetables.

Cooking Meat

When roasting meat it is a good idea to wrap it in tinfoil or use a roasting tray with a foil lid. By doing this, the meat will cook evenly with no risk of burning, and all the delicious cooking juices will be collected in the foil or tin, rather than collect at the bottom of the glass bowl. Half-way through cooking and once there is a build up of the juices, turn the meat over. This allows all the juices to filter down through the meat, basting it as it goes! This is very important as it helps keep the meat succulent and moist without the need for constant basting.

Gammon Steaks
• 2 gammon steaks. Serves 2
Preheat the Halogen Oven to 200°C as directed in the manufacturer's instructions.

Place the gammon steaks in a small roasting tin that will fit on the high cooking rack. Coat the steaks with olive oil and cook it for 10 minutes. The steaks will be moist and tender, but if you prefer a dryer finish, cook for a further 5 minutes.

Bacon
• 4-6 bacon rashers. Serves 2
You do not need to preheat the Halogen Oven.

Arrange the rashers of bacon on the high cooking rack. Set the temperature to 250°C and cook for 10 minutes. For crispy bacon, cook for a further 2 or 3 minutes. Turn the bacon over half-way through the cooking time.

Roast Beef

- 3kg (1.5lb) joint of beef such as silverside which has a small amount of fat within the meat to keep it tender. Serves 4-6

Preheat the Halogen Oven to 175°C.
Place the beef joint in a roasting tin. Drizzle olive oil over the top. Cover and seal the meat in the tin with a layer of tinfoil. Start cooking in three 30-minute stages for a total of 90 minutes. After each stage turn the beef joint over. At the end of the cooking time allow the meat to stand for 15-20 minutes.

Fillet Steak

- 1 fillet steak about 1/2 inch thick per person

There is no need to preheat the Halogen Oven.

Place the fillet steak in a small roasting tin. Cover the steak with a few grinds of black pepper and a drizzle of olive oil. Cook on 200°C. As a general guide, 8-10 minutes for rare, 10-15 minutes for medium and approximately 20 minutes for a well done steak. The steak can be turned over half-way through the cooking time.

Chicken

- 1 chicken fillet of breast/thigh per person.

There is no need to preheat the Halogen Oven.

Any chicken portion with skin on can be roasted on the high cooking rack without the need for a casserole dish, and simply brushed with olive oil. Chicken without a skin will benefit from being placed in a small casserole dish with a small drizzle of olive oil which will help prevent the meat from drying out. A seasoning of salt and black pepper will help bring out the flavour. Cook on 200°C for 15-20 minutes or until the meat in the middle is white, piping hot, tender, and the juices run clear.

Vegetable Pasta Bake

A hearty meal full of goodness.

- Serves 2
- Use a low cooking rack
- You will need a casserole dish

Ingredients

- 200g (7oz) penne pasta
- 400g (14oz) tin of chopped tomatoes
- 1 medium head of broccoli chopped into florets
- 200g (7oz) tin kidney beans
- 1 yellow pepper, deseeded and sliced
- 150ml (5.5floz) double cream
- 100g (3.5oz) grated cheddar
- salt and black pepper

Method

Preheat the Halogen Oven to 200°C as directed in the manufacturer's instructions.

Boil the pasta as directed by the packet instructions. For the last 3 minutes add the chopped broccoli. Drain and put back into the pan.

Stir in all the remaining ingredients except for the cheese; season it with salt and black pepper and put into a casserole dish. Sprinkle the cheese on top and bake for 20 minutes or until golden brown. If the top is browning too quickly a sheet of tinfoil can be placed over the dish until the end of cooking time.

Quick and Easy Pasta

An incredibly easy and hassle-free supper.

- Serves 2
- Use a low cooking rack
- You will need a casserole dish

Ingredients

- 200g (7oz) penne pasta
- 2 medium free range eggs
- 2 tbsp double cream

- 100g (3.5oz) gruyere cheese, broken into chunks.
- salt and black pepper

Method

Preheat the Halogen Oven to 180°C as directed in the manufacturer's instructions.

Boil the pasta as directed by the packet instructions. Drain the pasta and put back into the pan. Allow to cool for a few minutes while you prepare the eggs.

Beat the eggs in a separate bowl, stir in the cream and add to the drained pasta. Don't stir too vigorously or the eggs could scramble; just gently fold them through.

Crumble the cheese all over the pasta, season with salt and black pepper and bake for 10-12 minutes until golden brown and the pasta on top is slightly crunchy.

Although this dish is deliciously simple as it is, you could add a chopped red chilli for heat and colour, or fried bacon cut into cubes . . . just experiment.

Roasted Peppers

A healthy and filling dinner.

- Serves 2
- Use a low cooking rack
- You will need a small casserole dish

Ingredients

- 1 pepper per person - chopped horizontally with the seeds scooped out
- 3 tbsp couscous
- 1 heaped tbsp cooked tinned lentils, drained
- juice of 1 lemon
- 1 clove of garlic, peeled and chopped
- 150ml (5floz) ready-made vegetable stock
- small handful of chopped parsley
- 25g (1oz) feta cheese, chopped into cubes
- salt and black pepper
- 2 tbsp olive oil

Method

Preheat the Halogen Oven to 200°C as directed in the manufacturer's instructions.

Season the peppers, drizzle with 1 tbsp of the oil, place in the casserole dish and roast for 15 minutes until soft and tender.

While the peppers are roasting, prepare the couscous stuffing. Pour the couscous into a bowl, add the lemon juice, garlic, and lentils. Pour the boiling stock over the couscous.

Cover with tinfoil and leave for 5 minutes while the couscous absorbs all the liquid.

Remove the foil and fluff up the couscous with a fork, ensuring the mixture is dry with no water still left to be absorbed, otherwise the mixture will be bland and stodgy. Stir through the remaining oil, chopped parsley and a few grinds of black pepper.

14

Tear off squares of tinfoil big enough to wrap each pepper and remove them to the foil. Spoon the mixture into each pepper, being careful not to overfill it, crumble over the feta, being as generous as you like, wrap up the peppers in the tinfoil and continue to roast for a further 15 minutes. When the 15 minutes is up, just open up the foil to expose the tops of the peppers and bake for a further 5 minutes to allow the feta to go golden brown and slightly crunchy. Serve with salad.

Top tip
Mixing in a chopped sprig of rosemary to the couscous mixture will add great flavour to the filling.

Broccoli and Mixed Cheese Quiche

A delicious way to use up leftover cheese!

- Serves 4-6
- Use a high cooking rack
- You will need a baking tray

Ingredients

- one 8 inch savoury flan case (can be bought ready-made)
- 115g (4oz) small broccoli florets
- 115g (4oz) mixed cheese, grated
- pinch of grated nutmeg
- black pepper
- 250ml (18 fl oz) double or whipping cream
- 2 eggs, beaten

Method

Preheat the Halogen Oven to 180°C as directed in the manufacturer's instructions.

Boil the broccoli in a small pan of boiling water until it is just soft.

Sprinkle the cheese into the flan case.

Arrange the cooked broccoli on top of the cheese.

Beat the two eggs, cream, nutmeg and pepper in a bowl and gently pour over the cheese and broccoli.

Cook at 180°C for 15 minutes or until the top of the quiche is golden.

Roast Chicken Dinner

A one-pot solution to a Sunday favourite.

• Serves 2
• Use a low cooking rack

Ingredients

• small or medium chicken
  (1.5 -2kg/ 3.3lb-4.4lb)
• 1 or 2 small onions chopped into
  quarters
• 4tbls olive oil

• 4 carrots chopped into chunky
  sticks
• 2 parsnips chopped into chunky
  sticks
• 4 small potatoes cut into quarters

Method

Preheat the Halogen Oven to 175°C as directed in the
manufacturer's instructions.

In a bowl, toss all the vegetables in olive oil, ensuring they are
all coated in the oil.

Place the chicken on the low cooking rack and arrange all the
vegetables around it. Coat the chicken in a little more oil; there
will be no need to baste the chicken later.

Leave to cook for 1$\frac{1}{2}$ hours. Check the chicken is cooked by
pushing a skewer through the middle to see if the juice runs
clear.

Top tip
Adding a few drops of soy sauce over the chicken skin helps get a roasted, brown colouring.

Mediterranean Chicken

Big flavours for little effort.

• Serves 2
• Use a low cooking rack
• You will need a casserole dish

Ingredients

• 4 medium sized chicken thighs
• handful of cherry tomatoes
• handful of new potatoes, chopped in half.

• handful of olives
• salt and black pepper
• approximately 4tbls olive oil

Method

Preheat the Halogen Oven to 180°C as directed in the manufacturer's instructions.

Place the potatoes, tomatoes and olives in the casserole dish, then place the chicken thighs on top. (You could add a few torn basil leaves for extra flavour).

Season with salt and black pepper and a small drizzle of olive oil. Bake for 1 hour, turning the chicken half-way through.

When the chicken is cooked, the meat will come away from the bone with little effort and the skin will be beautifully crisp and sticky.

Chicken Escalopes

Chicken in a crispy breadcrumb coating.

- Serves 2 • Use a low cooking rack
- You will need a casserole dish

Ingredients

- 2 chicken breast fillets
- 2 tbsp plain flour
- 1 egg, beaten
- 4 tbsp breadcrumbs
- 2 tomatoes, roughly chopped
- 1 clove garlic
- a few basil leaves, chopped
- 2 tbsp olive oil
- 100g (3.5oz) mozzarella
- salt and black pepper

Method

Preheat the oven to 200°C as directed in the manufacturer's instructions.

Lay the fillets on a chopping board and cut through the middle horizontally, without going all the way through. Fold back the top layer to open out the fillet. Doing this will help it cook much more quickly.

Arrange three small plates, one with flour, one with the beaten egg and one with breadcrumbs. Season the flour, then coat the chicken, ensuring an even coverage; dust off any excess. Dip the fillet into the egg, followed by the breadcrumbs and coat evenly on each side. Repeat for the other chicken fillet.

Place the chicken in the casserole dish and cook in the oven for 10 minutes while you prepare the sauce. Mix the tomato, basil, garlic and 1 tbsp of the oil. Season with salt and black pepper and mix. Turn the chicken fillets over in the oven and spoon the tomato mixture on top. Tear up the mozzarella over each chicken fillet, add the remainder of the oil, and continue to bake for a further 15 minutes or until golden brown and the cheese is slightly bubbling.

Pork Steaks with Honey-Glazed Apple Slices

A simple idea that tastes as good as it looks.

• Serves 2
• Use a low cooking rack

Ingredients

• 2 pork steaks
• 2 apples, finely sliced
• runny honey (the bottle type)

Method

Preheat the Halogen Oven to 200°C as directed in the manufacturer's instructions.

Place the two pork steaks on the high cooking rack and set the timer for 20 minutes. Begin cooking.

After ten minutes turn the steaks over and cover with the apple slices. Drizzle honey over the apple slices.

Continue cooking for the remaining ten minutes.

Marinated Pork Chops

For maximum flavour, prepare a day in advance.

- Serves 2
- Use a high cooking rack
- You will need a casserole dish

Ingredients

- 2 pork chops
- 2 cloves garlic, unpeeled and lightly crushed
- 2 tbsp sesame oil
- 1-2 fresh red chillies, de-seeded and chopped
- 1 tbsp soy sauce
- Salt and black pepper

Method

Put all the ingredients into a dish. Cover with foil and leave to marinate in the fridge overnight, or a minimum of 45 minutes.

When you are ready to cook your pork chops, preheat the oven to 180°C.

Remove the marinated mixture from the fridge and remove the foil. Cook in the preheated oven for 15 minutes, turning the meat over half-way through. Great served with chips, mash, rice or salad.

Top tip
Adding a little fresh
rosemary and thyme to
the marinade will really
enhance the flavour, smell
and appearance of your
dish.

Beef Casserole

With or without the mashed potato topping, this recipe is a s-mash hit!

- Serves 2
- Use a low cooking rack
- You will need a casserole dish

Ingredients

- 400g (14oz) braising steak
- 2 large carrots
- 1 leek
- 1 butternut squash
- 300g (11oz) new potatoes
- 1 medium onion
- salt and black pepper
- 400ml (14floz) beef stock
- 150ml (5.5floz) red wine (optional)

Method

Preheat the Halogen Oven to 200°C as directed in the manufacturer's instructions.

Chop the beef and vegetables into 2-3cm (1 inch) chunks and season generously with salt and black pepper; then place in the casserole dish and cook for several minutes to lightly brown the ingredients. If using wine add it now.

Cook through for 4-5 minutes, or until the wine has mostly evaporated.

Add the stock to the casserole, ensuring all the vegetables and meat are covered.

Cook for 60 minutes, stirring every 10 minutes.

The casserole is ready to eat when the vegetables and the meat are tender. Season and serve.

Why not add a mashed potato topping to your casserole?

Ingredients

- 3-4 medium Maris Piper potatoes
- salt and black pepper
- 25g (1oz) salted butter
- 100g (3.5oz) grated cheddar
- 1 large egg yolk

Method

While the casserole is cooking, cut the potatoes into bite-sized chunks and add to a pan of salted boiling water.

Boil for 10-15 minutes or until the potatoes are tender. The potatoes are ready when a knife passes through them smoothly.

Drain the potatoes and put them back into the pan.

Add the butter and mash the potato until smooth. Add 3/4 of the cheese, the egg yolk, a pinch of salt and black pepper, and stir through.

Approximately 15 minutes before the end of cooking time, remove the dish and spread the potato mixture on top. Add the remaining cheese on top, fluff with a fork and bake for 10-15 minutes until golden brown.

Roast Beef with Roasted Vegetables

This method takes the stress out of getting all the vegetables ready at the same time.

• Serves 2-3
• Use the low cooking rack

Ingredients

• 3lb (1.5kg) beef joint such as silverside
• 3-4 carrots
• 3-4 potatoes
• 1 parsnip
• 1 head of broccoli
• 1 onion or 4 shallots
• a few drops of soy sauce (optional)

Method

Preheat the Halogen Oven to 200°C as directed in the manufacturer's instructions.

Brown each side of the beef in a frying pan in a small amount of oil. If a hob isn't available put the beef straight into a roasting tin and cover with a lid of tinfoil. Place the beef on the low cooking rack and cook for 30 minutes.

Cut all the vegetables into similar sized pieces. Cut the carrots and parsnips lengthways, then again into 4cm (2 inch) pieces.

The onion can be cut into 4 pieces and the shallots can be either left whole or cut in two.

Put the vegetables, except the broccoli, into a bowl. Cover with 3 tbsp of olive oil and sprinkle a few drops of soy sauce over them. Mix well, so that the vegetables are covered in the dressing.

After the first 30 minutes, place the vegetables into the bottom of the Halogen Oven around the outside of the low cooking rack. Turn the meat over in its roasting tin, replace the foil and cook for a further 30 minutes.

Meanwhile, cut the broccoli into small florets and wrap in tinfoil, adding 2 tbsp of water; add this tinfoil parcel to the oven. Stir the vegetables. Turn and baste the meat once more. Cook for a final 30 minutes, then remove the meat dish. Keep the meat covered but allow it to 'rest' for about 15 minutes before carving.

Test the vegetables with a fork to see if they are cooked. If they are, turn the temperature down to 100C to keep them warm. While the meat is resting, you will have time to make gravy and even pop a few ready-made Yorkshire puddings into the oven. They will only take 2/3 minutes to heat through.

Homemade Burgers

Easier than you may think!

- Makes 4 burgers
- Use a low cooking rack
- You will need a baking tray

Ingredients

- 500g (18oz) beef mince
- 1 onion, finely chopped
- pinch of cumin and coriander (optional)
- 2 heaped tsp of Dijon mustard
- 1 tbsp tomato ketchup
- 1 medium egg
- 5 tbsp breadcrumbs
- salt and black pepper

Method

Preheat the oven to 200°C as directed in the manufacturer's instructions.

Put all the ingredients into a large bowl and mix with your hands until it's all incorporated. Add more breadcrumbs if it's too sticky and wet: you want a nice smooth patty. If you are not using the mixture straightaway it can be covered in tinfoil and left in the fridge for up to two days.

Mould and roll the mixture into 4 round patties and place on a baking tray on the low cooking rack. Bake in the oven for 20 minutes, carefully turning over half-way through.

If you want to check that they're done, cut one in half to ensure the meat is no longer pink, but has turned brown.

Serve in toasted burger buns with salad.

Tartiflette

A creamy and indulgent French dish.

• Serves 2 • Use a low cooking rack
• You will need a casserole dish

Ingredients

• 3 medium Maris Piper potatoes
• 2 thick rashes of bacon
• 1 medium onion
• 60g (2oz) soft, creamy cheese such as Reblochon cut into cubes

• 200ml (7 fl oz) double cream
• 100ml (3.5floz) milk
• Salt and black pepper
• 2 tbsp bread crumbs (optional)
• 1 tbsp of grated Parmesan (or Cheddar)

Method

Preheat the Halogen Oven to 200°C as directed in the manufacturer's instructions. Put the casserole dish in the oven to warm.

Peel and finely slice the potatoes. Add to a pan of boiling salted water for 4-5 minutes until slightly tender. Drain, set aside and keep warm.

Meanwhile, cut the bacon into cubes and place in the hot casserole dish with a drizzle of olive oil. Cook for 2-3 minutes. Peel, roughly chop and add the onion. Stir.

When the onion is soft but not browned and the bacon is becoming crisp, add all the potatoes and arrange them on top. Cook for a further 5 minutes to add a little colour.

Add the cheese to the dish and season all over. Mix the milk and cream and pour over, then grate over the Parmesan. Bake for 60 minutes adding the breadcrumbs on top for the last 5 minutes if you're using them. If it's cooking too quickly on top, add a square of tinfoil.

Top tip
Take a broccoli head and cut into small florets. Wrap in tinfoil adding a tbsp of water. Place in the bottom of the oven and cook at the same time as the fish.

Baked Cod

Perfect, flaky cod every time.

• Serves 2   • Use a high cooking rack
• You will need a baking tray

Ingredients

• 2 cod steaks
• 1 tomato or 2 tbsp chopped
  sundried tomatoes
• Small packet of lemon and thyme
  stuffing

• 115g (4oz) grated cheese
  (Cheddar, Edam or Red Leicester
  work well)

Method

Preheat the Halogen Oven to 200°C as directed in the
manufacturer's instructions.

Place the cod steaks on a small baking tray lined with tinfoil.
Cover the fish in thin slices of tomato. Sprinkle the dry stuffing
mix over the top of the fish, followed by the cheese.

Bake for 15 minutes on the high cooking rack until the fish
breaks into flakes.

Or why not try . . .

Salmon with Parsley Butter

Preheat the Halogen Oven to 200°C as directed in the
manufacturer's instructions.

Take 2 salmon fillets. Mix freshly chopped parsley into a tbsp
of softened butter. Spread the butter over the fillets, place them
into a small ovenproof dish and cook on the high cooking rack,
for 10 minutes.

Salmon with Ratatouille

A complete meal, full of colour and flavour.

• Serves 2   • Use a low cooking rack
• You will need a small casserole dish

Ingredients

• 2 salmon fillets
• 1 medium red onion, peeled and chopped
• 1 courgette, diced
• 1 aubergine, deseeded and diced
• 1 red pepper, deseeded and diced.
• 400g (14oz) tin of chopped tomatoes

• juice of 1 lemon
• 1 glass white wine
• pinch of sugar
• salt and black pepper
• 4 tbsp olive oil
• handful of fresh basil leaves (optional)

Method

Preheat the Halogen Oven to 200°C as directed in the manufacturer's instructions.

Pour half the oil into the casserole dish and place in the oven while you prepare the vegetables. Season the salmon with salt and black pepper and put in the fridge.

Add the onion to the casserole dish and stir to coat in the oil; cook for 4-5 minutes. Add the courgette and aubergine along with the remaining oil and stir well. Cook for a further 8 minutes, stirring now and then until the vegetables are becoming tender. Add the pepper, tomatoes, sugar, lemon juice, wine and basil leaves if you're using them and stir. Cook for approximately 25 minutes, stirring occasionally until the sauce has thickened and the vegetables are soft.

Remove the seasoned salmon from the fridge and place on top of the sauce, skin side up. Cook for a further 8 minutes, turning the salmon over half-way through.

Something Tasty On Toast

If you need a snack in a hurry, a topping on toast is ideal. This method is easier than using a grill and much less likely to burn!

• Serves 1-2 • Use a high cooking rack

Ingredients

• 2 slices of bread   • 2oz grated cheese (Cheddar)   • 1 sliced tomato

Method

There is no need to preheat the Halogen Oven for this recipe.

Put 2 slices of bread on the high cooking rack. Cover with tomato, then the grated cheese. Cook for 5 minutes on 200°C.

Here are a few more ideas, but there really is no limit:
 • Try different cheese combinations such as Edam and Cheshire, Dolchelatte and Cheddar, Stilton and Cheddar
 • Sliced mushrooms, with tomato.
 • Slices of pepperoni, tomatoes and cheese.
 • Tapenade and goats' cheese.
 • Thinly chopped ham, tomatoes and grated cheese.
 • Tinned baked beans. No need to pre-heat the beans in a pan. Cook the bread slices for 2 minutes, then spoon the beans onto the toast and cook for a further 3 minutes.
 • Tinned chilli con carne, slices of fresh tomato topped with grated cheese. Heat the bread for 1 min, spread with the chilli con carne, cook for 2 minutes. Add the tomatoes and cheese. Cook for 2 minutes.
 • Grated onion and cheese.

Welsh Rarebit

The perfect tasty topping for toast.

- Makes enough to cover 6 slices of toast
- Use a high cooking rack

Ingredients

- 25g (1oz) butter
- 25g (1oz) plain flour
- 150ml (5fl oz) milk or 300ml (10fl oz) if not using beer
- 150ml (5fl oz) beer, such as brown ale (optional)

- 175g (6oz) grated cheese
- 2 egg yolks, beaten
- 3-4 drops Worcester sauce
- 1/4 tsp dry English mustard
- salt and black pepper

Method

There is no need to preheat the Halogen Oven for this recipe.

Melt the butter on a low heat, add the flour and mustard and stir the mixture well. Add all the liquid very gradually, stirring all the time. The mixture will thicken.

Now add the beaten egg yolks and the cheese and blend to a smooth, thick mixture.

Spoon generous amounts of the mixture onto thick bread and cook on the high cooking rack for 4-5 minutes on 250°C.

You can toast one side of the bread first for a crunchier result by placing slices of bread on the high cooking rack for 2 minutes, then turn the bread over before adding the Welsh Rarebit mixture.

Top tip
The Rarebit
mixture can be
frozen and stored
for 2-3 months.

Top tip
Mix the milk and the
cream in a saucepan and heat
gently to a gradual boil before
mixing with the potatoes. Adding
some chopped herbs and garlic
at this stage will add an extra
dimension to the overall flavour.

Potato Dauphinoise

A great accompanying dish for meat, fish or vegetables.

- Serves 4
- Use a low cooking rack
- You will need a casserole dish

Ingredients

- 5 medium Maris Piper potatoes
- 350ml (12floz) cream
- 350ml (12floz) milk
- 80g (3oz) Gruyére cheese
  (Cheddar will also work)
- salt and black pepper

Method

Preheat the Halogen Oven to 200°C as directed in the manufacturer's instructions.

Peel and finely slice the potatoes. Mix the milk and cream together.

Layer half the potatoes in a casserole dish, cover with half the milk and cream mixture, sprinkle over half the cheese, and season with salt and black pepper. Repeat this process with the remaining ingredients.

Bake for 60 minutes until golden brown and the potatoes are nice and tender and the milk and cream mixture has thickened.

Olive Bread

Great for parties or as a tasty snack.

- Serves 4-6
- Use a low cooking rack
- You will need a baking tray

Ingredients

- 500g (18oz) strong white plain flour; the better the quality, the better the flavour
- 7g sachet dried yeast
- 1tsp salt
- 325ml (11floz) lukewarm water
- 2 tbsp extra virgin olive oil

For the Olive Spread
- 150g (5.5oz) pitted black olives
- 1 tbsp olive oil
- black pepper to season
- 1 heaped tsp paprika (optional)
- 2 cloves of garlic (optional)
- a few basil leaves (optional)

Method

Sieve the flour and salt into a large bowl, add the dried yeast and mix, then make a well in the centre. Mix the water and olive oil, and pour a little into the well, mixing with a fork. When the mixture becomes dry, add a little more water and continue until the water has gone.

Lightly flour a work surface and turn the mixture out onto it. Knead the mixture until you have a soft and springy dough, a minimum of 5 minutes; however, there is no set method; twist, pull, push and squeeze! Place the dough in a large bowl, cover with cling film and leave in a warm place for 2 hours and until it has doubled in size.

After 2 hours, lightly knead the dough again to squeeze out excess air. Wrap in cling film and leave it in the fridge while you prepare the olive mixture.

Preheat the Halogen Oven to 200°C as directed in the manufacturer's instructions.

Place all the ingredients in a bowl, crushing and mixing with a fork until you have a rough spread. Set aside. Roll out the dough to a thickness of about 1cm (1/2 inch) and into a long rectangular shape. Spread the olive mixture on top of the dough, going right up to the edges.

Starting from the edge nearest to you, gently roll up the dough, creating a Swiss roll effect. Trim a few centimetres off each edge and then cut into slices of approximately 5-6 cm (2 inches) in thickness. You should have about 5 slices. Place on a baking tray. Season with pepper and bake for 15 minutes until golden brown.

Top tip
For extra crispiness coat the potatoes in semolina flour between parboiling and putting them in the oven.

Roast Potatoes

The perfect accompaniment to any roast dinner.

• Serves 4

Ingredients

• 4 large potatoes
• vegetable oil

• 1 tbsp soy sauce

Method

Preheat the Halogen Oven to 200°C as directed in the manufacturer's instructions.

Peel the potatoes and cut them into even-sized pieces. Parboil the potatoes, drain them and allow them to cool.

Pour enough oil to cover the bottom of the oven and re-heat for another 5 minutes.

Add the potatoes and sprinkle with soy sauce. Cook the potatoes for approximately 1 hour or until the potatoes are golden brown.

Cheesy Biscuits

Moreish nibbles, great with a glass of wine!

- Makes approximately 16 biscuits
- Use a high cooking rack
- You will need a baking tray

Ingredients

- 115g (4oz) whole wheat flour
- 115g (4oz) butter
- 1/2 tsp salt
- 1/4 tsp black pepper
- pinch cayenne pepper or English mustard powder
- 115g (4oz) grated Cheddar cheese
- 115g (4oz) grated Parmesan cheese

Method

Preheat the Halogen Oven to 175°C as directed in the manufacturer's instructions.

Rub the butter into the flour and add the salt, black pepper and either the cayenne pepper or English mustard powder.

Add the cheeses and mix well to make a dough (a food processor can be used at this stage).

Shape the dough into a thick roll, about 10 inches long. Place the roll on a tray and pop into the freezer for 20 minutes to make the dough firm.

After 20 minutes, take the dough out of the freezer and cut into thin, even slices to make the biscuits.

Place on a greased or lined baking tray and bake for 8-10 minutes. You will need to cook the biscuits in two batches. Let the biscuits cool for 10 minutes to become firm.

Apple and Blackberry Bake

Delicious served with custard or ice-cream.

- Serves 6
- Use a low cooking rack
- You will need an oven-proof dish

Ingredients

- 6 apples, peeled and sliced
- 140g (5oz) blackberries
- 60g (2oz) caster sugar

For the Topping:
- 115g (4oz) self-raising flour
- 1 tsp cinnamon
- 60g (2oz) softened butter
- 60g (2oz) caster sugar
- 1 egg beaten
- 3 tbsp of milk

Method

Preheat the Halogen Oven to 200°C as directed in the manufacturer's instructions.

Soften the apple slices in a pan with the caster sugar and a tbsp of water; keep on a low heat so they don't burn.

While the apples are softening, prepare the topping by mixing all the ingredients together to form a thick batter. This stage can be achieved using a food processor or a large mixing bowl and some vigorous stirring.

Place the softened apples in the oven-proof dish and sprinkle with the blackberries. Drop spoonfuls of the batter mix over the fruit.

Bake for 15-20 minutes or until the top is golden brown and firm to touch.

Cupcakes

Fluffy, golden and great with a cup of tea!

- Makes approximately 12 cupcakes
- Use a low cooking rack
- You will need a cupcake tray that will fit into the Halogen Oven.

Ingredients

- 110g (4oz) self-raising flour, sifted
- 110g (4oz) caster sugar, sifted
- 110g (4oz) unsalted butter or margarine
- 2 large, free range eggs
- 1tsp vanilla extract
- 1tsp baking powder
- icing and decorations; these can be bought ready-made

Method

Preheat the Halogen Oven to 200°C as directed in the manufacturer's instructions. Put the cupcake cases into the cupcake tray.

Put the sugar and the fat into a large bowl, then, using either a hand whisk or an electric whisk, beat the mixture until smooth.

Add half the flour and beat the mixture well before adding one egg, beating the mixture until smooth. Repeat this process with the remaining flour and egg. Add the baking powder and the vanilla extract. Beat the mixture to a smooth consistency.

Spoon the mixture into the cases using about 2-3 tsp of the mixture for each case.

Bake for 12 minutes. The cupcakes are ready when they are firm but slightly bouncy to the touch, or when a skewer is placed into the middle of the cake and it comes out clean.

Afternoon Tea Scones

An English classic that is easy in a Halogen Oven

• Makes approximately 8-10 scones
• Use a high cooking rack   • You will need a baking tray

Ingredients

• 225g (8oz) self-raising flour
• 1/2 tsp salt
• 1 tsp baking powder
• 60g (2oz) butter

• 1/4 pint milk (or half milk and half sour cream)
• 1 tbsp caster sugar
• 1 beaten egg to glaze (optional)

Method

Preheat the Halogen Oven to 200°C as directed in the manufacturer's instructions. Grease the baking tray.

Rub the butter into the flour, salt and baking powder to make a crumbly mixture which resembles breadcrumbs.

Add the milk gradually until the mixture starts to stick together into one big ball.

Shape and pat it into a 1/2 inch slab, using your hands not a rolling pin, in order to keep the dough light.

Cut 8-10 scones out of the mixture with a round pastry cutter, about 2 inches in diameter.

Place the scones on the pre-greased baking tray and glaze with beaten egg.
Place the tray on the high cooking rack and cook for 10 minutes.

Remove the scones and allow to cool for 10 minutes before cutting in two and serving with cream and jam.

Mincemeat and Apple Slice

This easy recipe can be eaten hot with cream or cold the next day as a lunch-time pudding.

- Serves 6
- Use a low cooking rack
- You will need a baking tray

Ingredients

- 175g (6oz) butter
- 75g (2.5oz) caster sugar
- 150g (5.5oz) plain flour
- 1tsp baking powder
- 2 egg yolks

For the Topping
- 400g (14oz) mincemeat
- 3 apples, sliced
- 50g (1.75oz) melted butter
- 3tbsp caster sugar

Method for the Base

Preheat the Halogen Oven to 200°C as directed in the manufacturer's instructions.

In either a bowl or a food processor, mix the butter, sugar, flour and baking powder and eggs until the mixture sticks together.

Press the mixture flat into a cake tin and bake for 10 minutes. Remove to a work-surface.

Method for the Topping

Spread the mincemeat over the cooked base. This is made easier if you warm the mincemeat for a few minutes first in your Halogen Oven. Lay the apple slices over the top of the mincemeat, overlapping the slices slightly.

Drizzle the melted butter over the apple and sprinkle with the sugar before baking for a further 10 minutes.

Conversion Charts

Oven Temperatures

Temperatures are guidelines only. Most food will be cooked between 175°C and 200°C. The standard highest setting of 250°C will be used to grill food in your Halogen Oven.

°C	°F
125	257
150	302
175	347
200	392
225	437
250	482

Liquid Measures

Metric	Imperial
30ml	1 fl oz
60ml	2 fl oz
100ml	3 fl oz
125ml	4 fl oz
150ml	5 fl oz
190ml	6 fl oz
250ml	8 fl oz
300ml	10 fl oz
500ml	16 fl oz

Dry Measures

Metric	Imperial
30g	1oz
60g	2oz
125g	4oz
185g	6oz
250g	8oz
315g	10oz
375g	12oz
400g	14oz
500g	16oz